TENANT LEASING 101:

The Essential Business and Legal Strategies for Your Next Lease

James P. Moorhead

TENANT LEASING 101:

The Essential Business and Legal Strategies for Your Next Lease

James P. Moorhead

in conjunction with

Moorhead Law Group
Attorneys & Counselors at Law

Nothing in this book should be considered as legal advice, and readers of this book should obtain such legal advice from their own counsel. This book is intended for education and informational purposes only.

ISBN-13: 978-1502954053

ISBN-10: 1502954052

For more information, please contact:
James P. Moorhead
Moorhead Law Group, LLC
321 North Clark Street
Fifth Floor
Chicago, IL 60654
(312) 445-6262
jmoorhead@moorhead-law.com
www.moorhead-law.com

Thanks very much to my family for their patience as I wrote this during too many early mornings, late nights, and weekend afternoons. Two big peaks, two little peaks, one fantastic family.

TABLE OF CONTENTS

TABLE OF CONTENTS

PREFACE

I have had the opportunity over the last fifteen years to work with all kinds of companies leasing property – from retailers, to corporations, to brand new start-ups. During all these transactions, I have come across virtually all types of prospective tenants.

This book was written for all of these kinds of tenants, from the highly experienced national company to the one just starting out. It is designed to be a useful roadmap for the next lease. People new to the lease process may find the broad directional guidance helpful. Experienced tenants may find the analysis of the more technical lease provisions useful.

The last few years have been challenging for all companies. It is my hope that this book will help companies with what is sure to be a major transaction for each of them. If the ideas, strategies, and tips in this book can make the leasing process just a little bit easier for these tenants, then it will have served its purpose.

James P. Moorhead
Founding Principal
Moorhead Law Group, LLC

October, 2014
Chicago, USA

ABOUT THE AUTHOR

I am the founding principal of the Moorhead Law Group, LLC in Chicago and run a national leasing practice for both tenants and landlords involving retail, office, manufacturing, restaurant, timber, resort, and industrial sites.

Award-Winning Attorney

Since 1999, my practice includes commercial real estate, land use, sports law, and conservation. Among others, I advise tenants, landlords, landowners, and athletes. I love working alongside clients and helping their businesses grow. I am comfortable counseling executives and general counsels of companies of any size. Clients include retailers, law firms, investment companies, manufacturers, and resort properties. I have handled roughly 750 leases and 300 purchases and sales in all 50 U.S. states, with a total value above $2 billion. I was selected as a "40 Under Forty Illinois Attorneys" by the Chicago Daily Law Bulletin in 2011.

Founder of Moorhead Law Group, LLC

I founded the firm in 2012 as a focused, hard-working law firm with a national practice in real estate, sports law, and conservation. We pride ourselves on a reasonable approach, responsiveness, and fair pricing. Formerly a partner in a large national firm, I believe that clients should not suffer unreasonable legal fees for high quality legal services. Clients note the firm's fair approach, sound advice, and ability to get transactions done on time, on budget, and without surprises.

For more information, please visit www.moorhead-law.com.

INTRODUCTION

Even though the national leasing market has improved in the last few years, proactive thinking remains the winning strategy in lease negotiations.

For retail tenants, it is not yet entirely clear whether the economy is back on track. Even if the customers are back ready to buy, retailers have to contend with online competition for each brick and mortar store.

A real estate lease is one of the biggest financial obligations of any company. It is usually second behind payroll. Whether a particular lease is for the first store a company is opening or is for the 1,000th store being opened, a company must review each lease to make sure it is sound from business and legal perspectives. It must also analyze each lease to confirm that it aligns with the company's business plan and strategic objectives.

Below is a set of ideas - suggestions based on my work experience and not an exhaustive or hard-and-fast set of rules - that might be considered in conjunction with reviewing a new lease agreement or an amendment to renew or extend an existing lease.

This book is not legal advice and does not replace the need to use an experienced lawyer for negotiating your lease. This book should be used as a guide for thinking through your transaction and as a roadmap for how it should go.

Best of luck on the success of your business.

CHAPTER ONE

WHERE TO START

Unless you plan to work from home or purchase a property for your business, you very likely will need to lease space for your company. If you already are in operation and are leasing space, you probably are aware of when your lease expires. For as long as you are leasing, you should be familiar will the fundamentals of leasing, including the general timeline for any typical lease negotiation. If you lease, taking the time to learn leasing fundamentals will pay off in dividends during the lease term.

Using a Broker

Unless you know the exact space that you want to lease and feel comfortable negotiating the lease terms, including tenant incentives and other benefits, it probably is a very good idea to use a real estate broker for your next lease. A good broker will know the properties in particular geographic areas, current rental rates, and what tenant incentives might be available. In short, a broker can help you secure the best economic package for your new lease.

Without basic knowledge, leasing space can feel very daunting.

Brokers often will specialize in particular types of property and geographic areas. There are brokers that specialize in office, retail, warehouse, or restaurant properties, and there are those who work in suburbs, downtown areas, and other markets. Picking the right broker for your transaction is an important process, and asking for referrals is a great way to meet the right person to help. It should be noted that broker commissions virtually always are paid by landlords.

Negotiating the Terms

Once you secure the right broker, that person will help you look at sites, compare rent and other lease economics, negotiate the final deal, and finalize a letter of intent. A letter of intent is a non-binding document listing the business terms of the proposed lease. It will include rent, term length, and extra costs like insurance, taxes, and building operating costs, and it will list any tenant incentives, including things like rent abatement and construction allowances.

Timing

Finding a site to lease can be a lengthy process, especially for retailers who need particularly good sites for customer traffic. Businesses should anticipate the length of this process, which generally can run from one to several months.

If you are starting a business, it will consume a large part of your start-up mental energy and focus. Be prepared for this, and reserve enough time to carefully review the entire deal, including additional costs and other terms that may drag down anticipated profit.

If you currently have a business and are leasing now, begin the next lease or renewal process with enough lead time so that you do not become a "captive tenant" in your existing space – finding yourself stuck at the end of your lease term without a deal for renewing or moving will make you feel (and appear) desperate and can hurt your negotiating leverage. Landlords probably will know your desperate situation and will take advantage of this in the deal making process.

Timing, planning, and good advice are three pillars upon which you can successfully navigate through a lease transaction and get back to focusing on your number one priority: the success of your business.

CHAPTER TWO

BEGINNING THE REVIEW

Once you and your broker sign the letter of intent, the landlord's attorney will send you a draft lease within a week or two. The complexity of the lease depends on the type of property. Generally speaking, retail leases are the most complex, with office leases being a bit more straightforward and warehouse leases being the most straightforward. Irrespective of the type of lease, they all seem to be getting longer over the years, particularly after the economic downturn of 2008.

When landlord sends you the lease, it easily could be 50 or more pages, especially with exhibits. For a person not in the real estate business, the lease can be a bit daunting. So, what do you do? Here's a brief list of action items:

Review Business Terms

As discussed later in more detail, the tenant should review the lease to confirm that the business terms reflect the agreement with landlord. The business principal will have the best knowledge regarding both the business deal and what is acceptable to the company. While the broker and lawyer will review these terms as well, the business owner is the only one who will be responsible to satisfy the terms, so it is worth the time to review.

Have Broker Review

Your broker is earning a hefty commission to get your lease done. As part of that fee, they should be taking an active involvement in the lease review and negotiation. A broker that simply puts together a letter of intent and is absent during the lease negotiation is not a benefit. Ask the broker to review and to provide feedback. The best brokers will review, prepare revisions to the draft, and will maintain an active involvement during the entire negotiation.

Hire a Lawyer to Review

Unless you are a lawyer or have an excellent understanding of the legal components to a lease, it is worth your time and money to hire a lawyer. A lawyer that focuses on leasing, particularly tenant leasing, will be able to help you negotiate the best deal and will help you navigate the subtle landmines in leases. Do not hesitate to negotiate the fee for your lease to have some scope of the overall cost.

Have Your Insurance Agent Review the Insurance Section

This often is overlooked, but your insurance agent should be brought into the lease process early. The best way to handle this is to cut and paste the insurance section of the lease right into an email to your agent. Having the agent review the terms and provide feedback will help you know what conflicts there are between your policy and the requirements of the lease. Handling this early will avoid any last minute problems before you are ready to sign.

A lease is a huge obligation – many last 10+ years and carry a sizeable rent amount. It usually is the first or second biggest obligation of a company (payroll being the other). There almost always are landmines to navigate in a 50-page lease. Utilizing and hiring the best team for your lease project will help get you the best deal and the most user-friendly document you can.

CHAPTER THREE

HIRING LEGAL HELP

When you are in the process of leasing commercial space, it is a very good idea to ask someone with a real estate law background to help review the document. Even short lease documents can have tricky provisions and legalese language that may not be as straightforward as they appear.

Hiring a lawyer can be an intimidating process, but here is a breakdown of some key points to consider when seeking legal help:

Work Experience

Some lawyers will claim to be real estate lawyers even if they never regularly practice in this area. These lawyers can be easy to spot – on their website biographies, they will list several unrelated areas of law, including real estate. These lawyers sometimes are great. Sometimes they are trouble. If your lease is of any significance (and real estate usually is the second biggest obligation of a company behind payroll), it is important to make sure your lawyer actually knows real estate. Do not be afraid to ask about specific work experience similar to your type of lease.

Properly hiring a lawyer requires some effort, but it can pay dividends.

Referrals

In addition to asking about specific work experience, asking trusted friends and business acquaintances for a referral is a good way to find a lawyer. Practicing law is both a legal profession and a relationship business. Ask your trusted friend both how the legal product was and how the relationship was. You want an attorney with whom you can work - not one that never calls you back, talks at you and not with you, or is intimidating. The right personal fit is important.

Cost

There are a million jokes about lawyers, and many of them are not without reason. Lawyers can be high priced, and you often will not know the final cost until you receive the bill. This can create a huge anxiety, particularly in a slow economy. Two recommendations are to ask for a fee estimate and budget up front and to ask the lawyer to cap the total legal fee. By asking for a fee estimate, you are better able to set your own budget for your company. It is wholly reasonable for lawyers to operate within agreed-upon budgets. Asking for a cap of fees is not unreasonable. If the level of legal representation is discussed in advance with the lawyer (the lawyer could do a light review or a detailed line-by-line legal analysis, or something in between), you both can better predict the type of legal work required and the resulting legal bill.

CHAPTER FOUR

REVIEWING THE BUSINESS TERMS

In any type of real estate lease – retail, office, restaurant, industrial, or any other kind – the business principals of the tenant should take the critical step of reviewing the business terms within the lease.

The tenant's broker also should review the lease to confirm that its terms comply with the agreed-upon letter of intent, and an attorney should do the same as a regular part of its lease review.

Even with these two layers of review, the business principals will be the only ones that truly know what the day-to-day operations will be like within the leased space. These principals will be the only ones who can serve as a backstop to make sure that the lease terms will not conflict with how they intend to use the space.

Here are some key provisions to double-check, even if the attorney and broker have signed-off:

- Double-check the rent calculations to see if they are correct.
- Review the square footage, unit number, street address, and the location of the premises on any site plan that is attached as an exhibit.

- Check the additional rent sections to see what 'rent extras' are added.

- Review any construction provisions.

- Review the default section to see if there is anything you cannot live with.

- Confirm the permitted signage is acceptable.

- If parking lot sales are needed, ensure this right is obtained.

- Are kitchenettes, coffee bars, or other amenities needed.

- Are there special IT closet or power and cooling needs.

- Does tenant require security doors for safety and confidentiality.

A tenant also needs to carefully review a prospective lease to make sure that its business strategy is reflected accurately within the agreement. A conscientious tenant will analyze a lease form to make sure the lease is aligned with its business plan, which may include checking the following:

- Term Length and Extension Rights.

- Termination, Contraction, and Expansion Rights.

- Permitted Uses, Assignment, and Subleasing.

- Delays in Delivery of Space and Holding Over.

A lease agreement generally is a tricky document to negotiate even in the most ordinary of circumstances. A lease requires the parties to negotiate terms that will bind landlord and tenant for many years into the future. By taking the time to review the business terms, a tenant will be able to more suitably protect itself under one of its biggest business obligations and keep its focus on the success of its business.

CHAPTER FIVE

SQUARE FOOTAGE, MEASUREMENTS, AND RENT CALCULATION

In leases, the rented space is measured on a square foot basis, and the rent is calculated on dollar-per-square-foot basis. This much is known and is pretty obvious to most people.

Drilling down a bit, office leases become more complicated when the question is asked: 'how is the square footage measured?'

In office leases (different standards can apply to retail, industrial, and residential leases, so we will stick to office space here for simplicity, even though this is good to know for all types of property), the leased area can be calculated in two ways. The first is 'Usable Area,' and the second is 'Rentable Area.'

Usable Area vs. Rentable Area

In basic terms, Usable Area and Rentable Area can be defined like this:

- Usable Area: This area is the actual physical area within the rented premises in which the tenant will operate. It is literally the space

Accurately measuring the square footage can affect the rental amount.

between the walls of the leased premises over which the tenant has exclusive control and possession. It can be helpful for a tenant to know this figure for purposes of planning the office layout, including locating workstations and furniture. This area is measured from the interior side of the common corridor walls, the inside of exterior building walls, and the middle of walls separating the leased area from adjoining tenant spaces. It does not include restrooms, elevator shafts, fire escapes, stairwells, electrical or mechanical rooms, janitorial closets, elevator lobbies, and public corridors.

- <u>Rentable Area</u>:   Rentable Area is the Usable Area plus a proportionate share of the elevator lobbies, restrooms, corridors, and other common areas in the building. This proportionate share is commonly called a 'Load Factor.' This Load Factor is generally calculated by dividing the total rentable area of the building by the total usable area of the building and typically is around 108-115%. The purpose of the Load Factor is to have the tenant pay for its proportionate share of the shared building space.

Rent Calculation

Rent is determined on a Rentable Area basis. This means that the annual base rent (not the common area expenses or other additional rent) is calculated by multiplying the Usable Area by the Load Factor, with the product (the Rentable Area) then being multiplied by the dollar-per-square-foot rent rate. One thing a prospective tenant should consider is that a building with a high Load Factor likely will cost the tenant more per square foot of Usable Area.

This is a very broad overview of a complicated topic. A safe recommendation is that any company looking to lease space should retain a skilled broker to help guide them through these complexities. A qualified broker will be a great aid in both analyzing an individual building and comparing one building to another.

CHAPTER SIX

TERM LENGTH AND ALTERNATIVES

The length of the lease term is a business decision that needs to be negotiated with the landlord, reviewed with the broker, and analyzed internally. It should be a length that makes sense with respect to the tenant's business and growth plan. It also should be a length for which the landlord will provide attractive economic and financial incentives. Finally, it should reflect current and anticipated economic realities for tenant by both mitigating risk and allowing for opportunity as they may arise during the lease term.

Preparing a long-term business plan can sometimes be an exercise in futility. A company may have a good grasp of its operations and plans for the next 3 months, or even 12 months. However, to accurately predict growth, opportunities, and challenges in two, five, or ten years can be virtually impossible. A business may find that one aspect of its business thrives while another does not.

Future global financial crises, technology advancements, weather and natural phenomenon, and government regulation all may impact a business in ways that cannot be predicted now.

The challenge for a prospective tenant is trying to use these plans and predictions as best as possible when signing a lease with a multi-year term, often five or ten years. Even though the business may experience dramatic change during the lease term, the rental and operational requirements will not similarly change or lessen during the term.

If a business cannot realistically and accurately predict where, how, or what it will be in one, five, or ten years, then a tenant should consider including provisions in its lease that will allow it to mitigate risk and seize on opportunities.

When deciding how long a lease term should be, a tenant will need to consider several factors, including the following:

Alignment with Tenant's Business Plan

A tenant should think through the parts of its business plan that it can control. Are the company executives intending to sell the company in the next few years? Are the owners planning to retire soon? Does the company need to follow a store opening growth plan to maintain a national presence, irrespective of whether individual stores operate at a loss? Is this a new business venture, which the owners are happy to wind down if not immediately profitable?

The term length should reflect the tenant's growth plan and tolerance for risk. A financially stable or growing business may be able to sign a ten year lease without a second thought. A family owned business, in which the patriarch is 75 and the family succession is unclear, may not need or want a lease with a ten year term and two renewal options.

Landlord Economic and Financial Incentives

A landlord may offer a few economic and financial incentives to attract a new tenant. Competitive base rent, additional rent caps and base years, and tenant improvement allowances could be included in the landlord's incentive package. The general rule of thumb is the longer the lease term, the better the incentive package. An experienced broker can help negotiate the incentive package for the prospective tenant.

Mitigating Risk

- Term Length: Some tenants currently are being very cautious about the length of new lease terms. In a strong economy, a tenant might not give much thought to signing a ten-year lease. However, some tenants who are concerned about the viability of their business or their success in a new market now may desire a shorter initial term with more renewal terms. In prior years, a lease could have a ten-year initial term and 2 five-year renewals. In today's market, that same deal might now have an initial three-year term and 5 three-year renewals. In this scenario, the tenant could get out of the lease deal if the business does not support the space but, at the same time, has reserved rights to the space if the business does well.

- <u>Reduction and Early Termination Rights</u>: If business is slow, having the right to reduce the amount of leased space or being able to exercise an early termination right (both are often with a fee paid to landlord) might be cost-effective methods to reduce the tenant's financial obligation and operational risk.

Seizing Opportunity

If business is better than expected, a right to expand into adjoining space is very useful for those who initially conservatively leased a smaller space due to the uncertainty of the business. With this right, a tenant could expand the amount of leased space by leasing adjacent space that would then become part of the leased premises.

A right of first refusal or a right of first offer are two additional provisions that an experienced lawyer or broker can negotiate into the lease to allow the tenant to expand if the business growth is better than expected.

By thinking through the lease term and aligning it with a realistic business and growth plan, the tenant can better help its business handle the unforeseen that inevitably arises during the lease term.

CHAPTER SEVEN

PERMITTED USES

The permitted use provision in a lease will state the specific things for which tenant can use the premises. An office landlord likely will limit the permitted use to office uses. A retail landlord will try to limit the permitted use section to only those specific uses that reflect the retail tenant's business.

How to Analyze the Permitted Use Section

A prospective tenant needs to keep a few things in mind with respect to this section. First, the permitted use needs to include the tenant's anticipated plans for the leased premises. If the tenant is a retailer and intends to sell women's shoes, this use must be included in the permitted use section.

Second, the permitted use section must not be too restrictive. If the prospective tenant wants to sell shoes for men, women, and children, it cannot accept a permitted use section that only provides for "women's shoe sales". This would be too specific and would severely impact tenant's operations.

Flexible permitted uses can help with consumer demand changes.

Third, the permitted use section must anticipate any future uses that the prospective tenant might want to include at the store. Even if the current permitted use is "women's shoe sales" and is acceptable now, the prospective tenant should consider if it might want to expand to other shoe sales, such as men's or children's. Since a lease is a multi-year commitment, the tenant needs to think through how its business might expand and evolve.

Finally, an ideal retail permitted use section would state a specific use and then would include "for any other lawful general retail use." This would be most flexible because it provides for any legal retail operation. This is not always acceptable to a landlord, but a savvy prospective tenant will try to insert this into its leases as a matter of good practice.

Broadly Worded Permitted Uses Benefit Subleasing and Assignment

A tenant should keep in mind that a broadly worded permitted use will help in the event it wants to sublease or assign the lease in the future. This may be particularly true if a business fails or underperforms and the tenant wants to quickly wind down the business and unload the lease obligation to a subtenant or assignee.

In conjunction with this, it is very important to make sure the permitted use definition is as all-encompassing as possible. For example, it is infinitely better to have a permitted use "for all retail uses" than a use only for "the sale of wicker furniture." A broadly-worded permitted use clause will expand the audience of prospective subtenants and assignees that can operate within it. A very narrow permitted use clause conversely may limit the size of the prospective subtenants that could use the space and might be interested in subletting. If tenant needs to rapidly end its operation at the site, a broad permitted use section is very helpful to secure during the lease negotiation as part of advanced preparation.

Prohibited Exclusives

At the same time the prospective tenant is reviewing the permitted use section, tenant also should review any prohibited uses listed in the lease. A retail landlord often will grant exclusive uses to other tenants and will list these exclusives as 'prohibited uses' in the tenant's lease. The review of the prohibited uses list should include checking to make sure the tenant's permitted uses are not prohibited. The review also should include consideration toward any potential future uses that tenant, or any potential future subtenants or assignees, may want to have in the store.

CHAPTER EIGHT

SECURITY DEPOSIT

A security deposit is the landlord's attempt to mitigate the risk of a tenant that cannot, or will not, honor its lease obligations. A landlord will review a prospective tenant's financial statements, operating history, and reputation to determine this risk.

Tenant's Business History Will Drive the Deposit Amount

If the prospective tenant's business is relatively new or its financial statements are not robust, this may drive a higher security deposit. If the tenant has had financial or operational troubles in the past, a landlord may want to hedge its risk by requiring a larger security deposit. A tenant with a history and reputation of damaging premises, poor maintenance, or other operating problems may be asked for a larger security deposit.

Tenant Should Request that Landlord Waive the Deposit

A prospective tenant first should try to negotiate out any type of security deposit in a lease. If the company has a national reputation or a strong business and financial track record, it may be a very desirable tenant for a landlord. In that case, the landlord may be willing to waive a security deposit in order to lure the tenant. This should be the tenant's first consideration regarding a security deposit.

What Kind of Deposit to Expect

If the tenant cannot have the security deposit deleted from the lease, it should expect a deposit amount equal to the base rent due for one to six months. The amount of the deposit will depend on all the risk factors listed above, as well as the customary practice of the geographic region of the leased premises. A landlord in New York City may require a higher deposit than one in Indianapolis, Indiana.

Other Terms to Negotiate

A tenant should insert a requirement that landlord is to refund the security deposit within 30 days. A landlord may counter with a longer period of time, but in any event, the landlord should be required to return the deposit within a defined time period. A tenant can attempt to have the deposit kept in a separate, interest bearing account, but whether or not a tenant will get this provision into a lease will often depend on tenant's negotiating leverage.

Letters of Credit

During the economic downturn after 2008, landlords were increasingly asking for a letter of credit (LC) as a security deposit because certain case law has held them to be more landlord-favorable during a tenant bankruptcy. These courts deemed the LC as a contract between landlord and the issuing bank and not a part of the bankrupt estate.

If the economy again becomes increasingly uncertain or if a landlord is nervous about the financial strength of the tenant, the prospective tenant should anticipate that a letter of credit might be required and should be aware that the LC probably will require additional time to negotiate. The negotiation will be between the landlord, tenant lawyers, and the issuing bank.

If time is of the essence with respect to a lease negotiation, the tenant should begin the LC process as soon as it is known that one will be required. By simultaneously negotiating the lease and the LC, the tenant may be able to shorten the overall time to complete and finalize the lease, allowing it to move forward to the construction and site opening phases.

CHAPTER NINE

BASE RENT

There are three main types of rent in leases: base rent, additional rent, and percentage rent. Depending on the lease, some or all of these rents may be included. Here is a quick summary of these three types:

- **Base Rent**: The annual rent paid for the right to the leasehold interest, which essentially is the right to the exclusive use and possession of the leased premises. This base rent will be a product of a variety of factors, including, among other things, fair market value, the length of term, and the size of premises.

- **Additional Rent**: This includes additional costs that a landlord and tenant agree are tenant's obligation. Usually, these additional rent costs are a proportionate share of common area expenses, landlord's insurance, and real estate taxes.

- **Percentage Rent**: Very simply, this is rent equal to a certain percentage of a retail store's gross sales.

Base rent seems to be fairly basic: tenant's obligation is to pay the amounts listed in the lease. However, as part of a lease review, it is important to spend a bit of time double-checking relevant base rent provisions. Some things to consider include:

Is It Gross, Modified Gross, or Triple Net?

- **Gross**: Under a gross lease, the tenant pays base rent and does not pay any additional rent. Landlord will pay the taxes, insurance and common area costs. Utilities may or may not be paid by tenant, and it is worth checking how these are handled. It generally is assumed that gross rental will be a bit higher than triple net or modified gross rent due to the fact that landlord is paying the additional rent charges.

- **Triple Net**: Tenant pays the base rent plus its proportionate share of common area expenses, landlord's insurance, and real estate taxes. The general idea is that the building's tenants are paying for all operating costs of the building.

- **Modified Gross**: This type can vary in design, but generally, tenant pays the base rent and also pays any increases in additional rent above the additional rent amount during the first year of the lease. The lease's first year usually is called the 'base year,' and tenant is obligated for increases over this base year.

How is the Rent Calculated?

Rent almost always is stated on a 'dollar per square foot' basis. If this $/sf amount is not specifically stated in the lease (i.e. only the rent amount is stated), it is helpful to insert the $/sf amount in case the leased premises are remeasured.

Additionally, all of the rent calculations should be checked to make sure that the per-square-foot rate multiplied by the square footage actually does equal the stated annual and monthly rent amounts.

How is the Rent Paid?

The annual rent should be paid in equal monthly installments. Otherwise, landlord could demand unequal amounts at various points of the year and disrupt tenant's cash flow. This is a minor, but important, point to check.

Right to Remeasure?

It generally is helpful to include a right to remeasure the leased premises. If tenant believes that there is a discrepancy between the actual square footage and the amount represented in the lease, tenant could have the premises remeasured. If the size of the premises really is smaller than as represented in the lease, the rent and any other cost based on a $/sf calculation should be reduced.

A helpful backstop to this is to have a 5% cap on any remeasurement to avoid a significant adverse effect if the premises are actually larger than as represented in the lease.

Generally, the rent provision is not subject to much negotiation in a lease review. However, it is worth spending a few minutes just to make sure that the provision is clear and accurate and does not place tenant in a disadvantaged position.

CHAPTER TEN

ADDITIONAL RENT TIPS

In a lease, additional rent usually is defined as any amount due to landlord by tenant over and above base rent. Depending on the lease, the big three additional rent items are (i) common area maintenance costs (CAM), (ii) real estate taxes, and (iii) landlord's insurance.

These additional rent costs are typically paid based on tenant's proportionate share of the entire center or building. Generally speaking, the proportionate share is equal to the square footage of the tenant's leased premises divided by the square footage of the building or center.

CAM, taxes, and insurance are highly technical, and their respective lease sections are complicated. This book cannot cover everything about them, and an experienced attorney should be consulted for the lease review. That said, here are a few tips for consideration:

Common Area Maintenance

CAM expenses are landlord's costs of operating the building or the shopping center of which the leased premises are a part and usually are passed to the tenants. The general rule of thumb for CAM is that the costs need to specifically relate to the operation of the building or center.

CAM should not include any costs relating to landlord's other properties or to its unrelated business expenses.

A prospective tenant should ask for and review historical CAM records. Typically, a tenant will request three years of CAM records. The specific costs should be checked, and the year-to-year trends should be analyzed as well to determine if the records can help predict what the cost increases will be. Among other things, unusual weather events – heat, snow, storms – may drive up costs.

Although a landlord may want to pass through all CAM expenses to tenants, certain expense items can, and should, be excluded. In addition to the summary of CAM expenses, the lease will (or should) have a list of costs specifically excluded from CAM. This list is important, and there are certain exclusions that are regularly included in leases. These include, among other things, certain capital expenses, items benefitting some but not all tenants, legal fees, and accounting fees not related to the particular property.

When representing retail tenants, approximately 25 items are on my list to push to exclude from CAM, and by negotiating these exclusions, tenant can help manage its expenses. The exclusions should be reviewed, and an experienced lawyer can add value with this section by making sure that the list of exclusions is as comprehensive as it can be.

Tenants have a variety of means to manage these costs, including base year provisions (tenant pays only the portion of CAM that is over and above the CAM amount in an agreed-upon base year) and caps on the amount that CAM expenses can increase annually.

A right to audit landlord's CAM calculations will help a tenant confirm that it is being charged accurately and fairly. In conjunction with this audit right, an enforcement mechanism – such as landlord being obligated for audit costs in the event there is a discrepancy of more than 2% - can be enough to encourage a landlord into keeping its books in proper order.

Real Estate Taxes

A prospective tenant needs to understand how the applicable jurisdiction collects real estate taxes. Some jurisdictions pay real estate taxes in arrears, some do not. If paid in arrears, the lease needs to state whether the tenant is obligated for the taxes assessed or the taxes due for any particular year. Most jurisdictions have real estate taxes online now, and in addition to looking at historical records, similar to CAM, the prospective tenant should become familiar with how taxes are paid.

Real estate taxes should not include income, franchise, estate, or transfer taxes. Transfer taxes are an important item to exclude. If the landlord ever were to sell the property without the transfer tax exclusion, it could theoretically pass those costs to the tenants. The base year provision used for CAM also can be used to manage real estate taxes.

With each lease, the question should be asked – "are there any unique things that need to be considered?" Two states in particular, Florida and California, have unique real estate tax issues.

Florida has a sales tax on real estate leases, which is unique to Florida and is paid by the tenant. California restricts the amount by which real estate taxes can increase year-to-year, but the property can be reassessed when landlord sells it. This means that a tenant may be relying on prior tax bills, but if landlord sells, the future taxes may be much higher. There are certain protections that one can negotiate into a lease to limit the risk in these situations.

Additionally, a tenant should receive the benefit of any real estate tax appeals, but the cost to tenant for such benefit should not exceed the amount of the reduction in taxes that the tenant receives.

Insurance

As mentioned previously, one of the best things to do with the insurance section is simply to copy and paste it into an email and then to send it to the tenant's risk manager or insurance representative to review. That person should be able to compare the lease's insurance section against tenant's existing or new policy.

The insurance representative also should be able to determine if the insurance requirements are reasonable or unreasonable. Often, a lease will have a boilerplate insurance section that is not entirely appropriate for the particular lease. Automobile, liquor liability, products liability, and completed operations are just a few types of insurance that may be included, even though they are appropriate for tenant's business. If certain provisions are not covered in the existing policy or are unreasonable, the negotiation can focus on having those items removed.

A landlord's attorney might claim that landlord is restricted from changing the insurance provisions due to covenants under its loan agreements. However, when pushed, the landlord's risk manager usually will find room to compromise.

It is much easier to deliver certificates of insurance instead of policies. If the lease requires delivery of an insurance policy to landlord, that should be changed in virtually every circumstance.

Insurance is a complicated section in any lease, and the advice and guidance of an experienced broker and attorney can help even a sophisticated tenant navigate its terms.

CHAPTER ELEVEN

PERCENTAGE RENT: UNDERSTANDING A TECHNICAL RETAIL LEASE PROVISION

In a retail lease, the three typical types of rent are base rent, additional rent, and percentage rent. Base rent and additional rent have been discussed earlier. Percentage rent is rent based on a percentage of the gross sales that tenant earns while operating its business at the site. Percentage rent may sound straightforward, but there are several things to consider in order to fully understand it.

Purpose of Percentage Rent

A retail landlord is spending time and money to make the shopping center as attractive as possible for customers. The goal of this effort is to maximize store sales for the tenants. In return, retail landlords desire to be compensated for the effort and will look to percentage rent as the way to receive a share of the store profits.

Definition

Percentage rent is calculated by multiplying an agreed-upon percentage by the amount of a store's gross sales that exceed a certain, pre-determined threshold. The agreed-upon percentage typically is 5-6% and is called the "percentage rent rate." The pre-determined threshold typically is the "natural breakpoint." This natural breakpoint will be the amount equal to the quotient obtained by dividing the annual base rent by the percentage rent rate.

Ancillary Benefits

When percentage rent is used, landlords may be willing to lower the monthly base rent amount. The thinking being that what a landlord may lose in base rent, it likely will make up based on store sales and percentage rent. If a company is nervous about opening in a new geographic area or in a new location, it may be worthwhile to consider thinking through the base rent-percentage rent structure. If a tenant secures a lower monthly base rent because of percentage rent and the store's sales then do not exceed the percentage rent breakpoint, this may be a cost-effective rental strategy for a tenant.

Exclusion from "Gross Sales"

In drafting percentage rent provisions, it is important for the parties to consider the types of sales that will be included in the calculation of gross sales. Just as specific items can be excluded from common area maintenance costs, specific items also can be excluded from gross sales. By excluding these items, the amount of gross sales will be reduced, as well as the amount of percentage rent that is calculated on these sales.

Calculating and Reporting

When reviewing a percentage rent provision, it also is important to consider the timing for the payment of the percentage rent. In an ideal percentage rent provision, the percentage rent is calculated and paid annually. If this is not possible, the lease then should state that the percentage rent is calculated annually and paid beginning in the month in which the natural breakpoint is met.

Some landlords will want the tenant to pay on a prorated basis for a partial year. This can be acceptable, but keep in mind that if a tenant opens its store just before the Thanksgiving and Christmas holidays, the gross sales could be unusually high during that period. This would unfairly trigger percentage rent and should be avoided or addressed.

A diligent tenant also may require that the gross sales reporting be done on a fiscal month basis, not a calendar month basis. Weekends typically have a higher sales volume than weekdays. Some calendar months have four weekends, and some have five. To address this inconsistency between months, the fiscal month calendar alternates between four week months and five week months. This fiscal month reporting will more accurately reflect the amount of gross sales during any given period of the year.

Landlord Requirements

To maximize the potential percentage rent payable to the landlord, a landlord might require the tenant to do a few things: continuously operate in the premises, not open another location in close proximity to the shopping center, and permit the landlord to audit the gross sales. Also, retail landlords may require gross sales reporting even if no percentage rent is required. The purpose of this is to keep close watch on the tenant's financial health and to anticipate finance-related problems.

This obviously can be a very complicated provision in the lease, and an appropriate attorney can be consulted for guidance.

CHAPTER TWELVE

TENANT IMPROVEMENT ALLOWANCES

A landlord likely will offer a prospective tenant financial incentives to secure the deal with them as a new tenant. As part of these financial incentives, the landlord may include a tenant improvement allowance. This is an amount of money that the landlord provides the tenant for its construction and decoration of the premises.

Payment

If tenant is receiving a tenant improvement allowance from landlord to build out its leased premises, tenant almost always will have to first pay for the construction costs before being reimbursed by landlord for the allowance amount. Tenant likely will have to provide the landlord with the appropriate lien waivers. The payment method can be negotiated. The allowance can be paid in installments or all at once. An often used approach is to have a payment made when construction begins, additional payments during the construction period as draws become necessary, with a final payment once the store opens.

Tenant improvement allowances can help make a good office look great.

Landlord Clawback

Tenants should be aware, however, of a landlord attempt to claw back the tenant improvement allowance in the form of overhead, supervisory, or other administrative fees in relation to the tenant's build-out. By prohibiting these charges in the lease, a tenant can protect itself from losing the true allowance value to these landlord fees.

Alternatives to Cash Allowances

It is worth noting that, although landlords might be inclined to provide competitive tenant improvement allowances to lure tenants, they may not have the available cash to provide this. Other options in lieu of an improvement allowance, or landlord agreeing to improve the premises, include adjustments to rent. In lieu of a tenant improvement allowance, tenant may be able to negotiate a lower monthly rent or a temporary rent abatement, which may result in a better lease deal to the tenant from a financial perspective. A broker can help negotiate these provisions.

Tenant Set Off Rights

As discussed, if tenant is receiving a tenant improvement allowance from landlord to build out its leased premises, tenant almost always will have to first pay for the construction costs before being reimbursed by landlord for the allowance amount. There is a risk that landlord may not reimburse tenant for these costs. Landlord may dispute the costs or may be short on funds because of financial difficulties. Having to carry these unexpected construction costs could be financially disastrous to a tenant.

Therefore, a tenant can protect itself by inserting a clause providing for a set off of the tenant improvement allowance against rent. If landlord does not reimburse tenant within a certain time period after tenant presents all required documents for reimbursement (e.g. 30 days), this clause would allow tenant to offset the tenant improvement allowance against rent coming due. A tenant should also be aware that any abatement for rent at the beginning of the term might delay receiving the benefit of this clause. This would mean that a tenant would not be fully reimbursed for construction costs until the construction costs can be fully applied to future rent coming due. However, it does provide for an efficient, non-litigation remedy for reimbursement of the allowance.

If tenant has the right to the offset the tenant improvement allowance against future rent, landlord may want to limit the amount a tenant can offset each month. The landlord may propose that tenant can only offset the tenant improvement allowance against 50% of the rent coming due each month. This would allow landlord to receive at least some cash flow each month. However, a provision like this creates a situation in which the tenant effectively is a lender to landlord for the construction costs and tenant improvement allowance, and the tenant should attempt to refuse this arrangement.

CHAPTER THIRTEEN

DELIVERY AND
DELAYED DELIVERY REMEDY

It normally is critical for a tenant to have new premises delivered by a landlord on time so that the tenant can open for business as scheduled and begin to generate revenue as budgeted. The premises should not be deemed delivered until landlord has fulfilled its requirements for delivery, and the rent commencement should not occur until, at least, delivery occurs.

The condition of the premises at the time landlord delivers the leased premises should be clearly stated in the lease. Ideally, the lease will say that landlord will deliver the premises with any landlord construction completed. The premises should be free of any other claims for tenancy or possession. There should not be any mechanics liens affecting the leased premises.

Landlord should be willing to state that the leased premises will not contain any hazardous substances. A helpful provision is to have landlord indemnify tenant from all costs and liability associated with the presence or removal of hazardous materials in and around the leased premises that were not introduced by the tenant. It also is helpful to have the lease state that the leased premises will be structurally sound, in good and proper working order, and in compliance with all laws, rules, and regulations, including the Americans with Disabilities Act. This will avoid any problems with building code or other issues that may delay receipt of a certificate of occupancy and will generally protect a tenant from any delays in opening its business.

The rent commencement should not occur until the leased premises are delivered to tenant with landlord's delivery obligations complete. Often, the lease will provide one of two things: a) a period of time between the date that landlord delivers and the rent commencement date to allow tenant to complete its construction in the leased premises, or b) a rent abatement period immediately after the rent commencement date to allow tenant to complete its build out without rent accruing.

For retail tenants, it is possible to also negotiate a free rent period if the rent commencement date were to occur during the Thanksgiving and Christmas holiday season. If tenant opens for business during this period, it will miss most of the benefit of the holiday sales by opening too late in the holiday season. It is therefore fair to the tenant either to not have to open the store in this period or to open but not pay rent.

Since it is critical for a tenant to have the leased premises delivered on time so the tenant can open for business as scheduled, the tenant should negotiate a remedy into the lease for late delivery. Typically, this remedy is a rent credit. If landlord were to fail to deliver the leased premises with landlord's work substantially complete by the set delivery date, tenant could receive one day of rent credit for each day of delay and two days of rent credit for each day after thirty days of delay. In addition, tenant can have a termination right if delivery does not occur after a period of time, as well as a reimbursement of tenant's out of pocket costs related to the lease.

CHAPTER FOURTEEN

TENANT'S ALTERATION RIGHTS

Generally speaking, a tenant should be allowed to have control over the aesthetic design and construction standards of its leased premises. Subject to a landlord's signage and construction requirements and certain prior approval from landlord, the tenant should be able to decorate, improve, and renovate its leased premises, storefront façade, and signage in such a way that tenant feels is necessary for its business operation.

Landlords typically will want to have review and approval rights over tenant alterations in the premises. The logic is straightforward: the landlord owns the building and wants to know what the tenant is doing to the building. That said, there are a few things to keep in mind:

- Landlord's review and consent should be reasonable. Landlord's review period should be a reasonable length that allows landlord to review the plans but is short enough to not delay tenant unnecessarily.

- Landlord's review and consent rights should be limited to structural changes and alterations affecting the roof and the exterior of the building. Structural alterations are, by their nature, significant alterations, and it is reasonable for landlord to have oversight. Often, if anyone but an authorized landlord party makes adjustments to the roof, the roof warranty could be automatically void, so it makes sense for a landlord to be involved when the roof is at issue. The exterior of the building is a significant item in retail leases because of the architectural and design standards for the retail centers. Tenants typically agree to landlord's review and consent rights for these types of items.

- Landlord should not have a review and consent right if tenant is only making cosmetic or non-structural alterations. Picture hanging, painting, new carpeting, and other similar items are relatively minor items, and a tenant should enjoy unfettered control and dominion over the interior of the leased premises. Sometimes this is negotiated as a cost threshold, such as 'tenant may make non-structural, cosmetic alterations costing less than $25,000.00 in the aggregate without landlord's consent.' Language like this usually is a reasonable why to compromise and to finalize this provision in the lease.

Landlord's review should be reasonable, and its consent should not be unreasonably withheld, conditioned, or delayed. The parties should be operating in good faith, and landlord should not be able to use its consent right as leverage for a separate matter.

Landlord review fees for reviewing the tenant's alterations ideally should be eliminated or capped. In any event, the potential cost should be contained. One way to contain the review fees is to limit them to landlord's actual out-of-pocket costs paid to third parties as part of its review and consent.

Tenant should have the right to abandon the improvements and fixtures at the end of the term. Tenant should have the right to remove its personal property and trade fixtures. If landlord insists on the right to have tenant remove the improvements at the end of the term, Landlord should only have the right to exercise this right at the time landlord grants its consent to the alteration. If landlord does not exercise its right at that time, then tenant should have the right to abandon.

CHAPTER FIFTEEN

LANDLORD'S MAINTENANCE REQUIREMENTS

There are a variety of maintenance and repair items with respect to the leased premises and the building or shopping center that need to be addressed in the lease. Several of these items should be landlord's responsibility, and a diligent tenant will address these items specifically in the lease to avoid any confusion or vagueness. Some things to consider for landlord's maintenance are the following:

Building Structure, Roof, and Utilities

During the term, the landlord generally should be obligated to maintain, repair and replace the structural elements of the building and to keep the roof water tight. Landlord ideally will be responsible for utility lines from the point of main connect to the point where such lines enter the leased premises and for life safety equipment and the sprinkler system.

Common Area Condition

Landlord should maintain and operate the common areas in a manner equal to the highest standard for buildings or centers of similar size and character in the geographic region in which the leased premises are located. This is important, particularly if the current landlord sells to a new party that may try to downgrade the quality of the building or center. The common areas should be maintained in compliance with all applicable law.

HVAC System

For office tenants, heating and air conditioning typically are provided from systems that serve the entire building. However, HVAC is a specific item that should be addressed for retail tenants because retail stores often have their own HVAC systems.

Ideally, the landlord will repair and replace the HVAC system as it becomes necessary during the lease term, but a landlord usually will not accept responsibility for both. Landlords typically will want the tenants to do the repairs. If the unit is new at the beginning of the term or is in exceptionally good repair, the landlord is much less likely to want to pay for a replacement during the term. The repair and replacement each are negotiable items, with the biggest factor being the age and condition of the HVAC unit.

A reasonable compromise is for the landlord to handle replacements and for the tenant to handle repairs. If the HVAC is new or almost new, the parties could agree to have the replacement cost amortized over its useful life, with the annual prorated cost paid by tenant. Landlord and tenant also could agree to a cap on tenant's repair cost obligation, over which landlord would pay. The HVAC unit is a major item, but careful negotiation between the parties should reach a suitable compromise.

Minimizing Disturbances

As a protective measure, it is useful to include a provision requiring landlord to perform its work while using its best efforts to minimize the disturbance of tenant's business. This will be a provision that tenant can raise in the event the construction interferes with the enjoyment of the premises or the access to or visibility of the leased premises.

Self Help

Another helpful provision is to provide tenant with the right to make landlord repairs in the event landlord does not timely do so, and tenant then can have an additional right to offset its repair costs against rent coming due. This type of self help provision may receive some pushback from landlord's attorney, but it is worth trying to negotiate into the lease.

Clearly articulating the maintenance, repair, and replacement responsibilities in the lease will avoid any confusion as these items inevitably arise during the term. The goal during the lease negotiation is to draft these sections clearly. Any confusion can lead to delay, business disturbance, and distraction from the tenant's focus on its business.

CHAPTER SIXTEEN

UTILITIES, TRASH, AND INTERRUPTIONS

Utilities, trash, and utility interruptions are three relatively straightforward topics, but they are important to understand because of how integral they are to a smooth business operation.

Who Provides?

For the utilities, it is important for the tenant and the landlord to discuss how the utilities are provided. Each landlord and each building seem to have a different method, so the tenant cannot assume it knows how it will be arranged. There are a handful of questions to ask:

- Are the leased premises separately metered?

- Will landlord arrange for the utilities, or does tenant have to do this?

- Will the utilities be stubbed to the wall of the leased premises, or does tenant have to connect at some other location?

- Who is responsible for utility maintenance, and at what point in the utility line does it become a landlord responsibility instead of a tenant's?

If the utilities are not separately metered, then tenant likely will pay them on a proportionate share basis, similar to additional rent. This is a reasonable approach. However, tenant should confirm that other tenants are not using a disproportionately high amount of electricity or water. If tenant pays its proportionate share on a square footage basis, tenant then would be paying an unfairly high amount. If the utilities are metered, the meters should installed at landlord's cost.

Adequate Capacity

Landlord should covenant in the lease that it will provide the utilities to the leased premises in sufficient capacity for tenant to operate its business. If the type of utility supply is critical to tenant's business, tenant can have the exact electric, lighting, or water specifications listed in the lease. Certain manufacturing, technology, or laboratory tenants may require such things.

Who Pays for Trash?

The tenant should always ask how the trash removal is handled. How often is it picked up? Is the cost included in the additional rent? Is it a separate charge? How and where is it stored prior to being picked up?

Knowing these items will help a tenant plan for a key operational component of its business.

Interruptions

As discussed in other chapters, the tenant could try to negotiate a rent abatement provision into the lease that would provide tenant with a rent abatement in the event the utilities are interrupted. For example, if the utility service is interrupted for 48 hours, then rent could automatically abate if landlord does not fix the problem within the 48 hours. Tenant also could try to negotiate a right to terminate the lease if the utility interruption is not cured within 30 days. These are very helpful provisions to have for the tenant because they usually will motivate a landlord to remedy the problem.

CHAPTER SEVENTEEN

EXCLUSIVE USES

If having a competitor in the same retail center would be detrimental to the tenant's business, the tenant could negotiate an exclusive use right into its lease for either the type of store or particular products that are sold.

The Exclusive Use Right

An exclusive use right essentially is a right to be the only tenant in the retail center that has the right to sell particular types of goods. For example, if the tenant sold pet supplies, it could secure an exclusive use right to be the only tenant in the center to sell pet supplies. This would prevent a competitor from leasing space in the same center and taking customer traffic and sales from the tenant.

Draft Clearly But Inclusively

The exclusive use should be drafted with enough clarity to allow the tenant to have an unmistakable claim to the right to sell the specific goods. An exclusive right to sell 'music' is not particularly clear and could refer to musical instruments, audio equipment, or records and cd's. The

Exclusive uses can help protect against aggressive competition.

exclusive use also should not be so specific that it could allow competitors to sell competitive goods. If a tenant is in the basket selling business and only secures an exclusive for the sale of wicker baskets, the tenant could lose sales to a competitor that sells non-wicker baskets.

Address Future Growth Plans

The tenant also needs to consider whether tenant will want to reserve an exclusive use right for later in the lease term to sell things that it does not currently sell. A tenant in the confectionary business might secure an exclusive to sell confectionaries. However, this tenant's five year business plan anticipates that the tenant will add gift cards and stationery to its business in a few years. This tenant may want to secure an exclusive for gift cards and stationery.

Will Time Render the Exclusive Use Useless?

An additional consideration is whether the exclusive use might become outdated during the lease term by technological advancements. An exclusive to sell tape cassettes or even compact disks would not have much value in a current lease. The right to sell computers might not address all of the new technology that is being made, including tablets, iwatches, and Google Glass. To protect the tenant, an exclusive right to sell 'computers' might be better drafted as an exclusive right to sell 'computers, computer-related technology, and any computer-related products that may replace or otherwise substitute for current computer products'. By carefully thinking through the exclusive use in this way, the tenant can better protect itself from losing the value of its exclusive use right and having it rendered virtually useless before the lease ends.

CHAPTER EIGHTEEN

SIGNAGE

As part of the lease negotiation process, the tenant should make sure it obtains landlord's approval for the type and design of signage that it needs, as well as the number and location of the signs.

Office Tenant Signage

An office tenant may need relatively minimal signage. Usually, the office tenant will want signage at its office door and directory signage in the lobby. Other signage for an office tenant could be elevator signage and exterior building signage. The type and amount of signage is dependent on the tenant's leverage with landlord, which basically is driven by the amount of square feet that the tenant will be leasing.

Retail Tenant Signage

For a retail tenant, signage is critical to the success of the store. It is imperative for the tenant to have storefront signage. A retail tenant may also want window, pylon, monument, blade, and directory signage. The lease provision for signage can be very specific, including terms relating to lighting and sign materials.

A retail tenant should attempt to have its intended signage preapproved by landlord or, at a minimum, have its prototype signage preliminarily approved as generally acceptable to landlord. This second type of approval would simply mean that tenant's signage appears to be within landlord's requirements, which would not be binding on landlord but can provide some comfort to the tenant.

Any type of approval will require the parties to review the signage and to discuss the finer points that sometimes raise problems. How will the signage be lit? Does the signage need to be lit after the store closes, and if so, for how long? Does the tenant get signage on the center's pylon sign or monument? Can the tenant decorate the store windows or door?

These types of questions and discussions will allow the parties to flush out any issues. This is important because, by addressing these issues early on, tenant will be in a better position to promote and market its store in accordance with its marketing and business plans.

CHAPTER NINETEEN

RADIUS RESTRICTIONS
AND PROHIBITED USES

A radius restriction is a restriction put in place by a landlord that charges percentage rent. The radius restriction prevents a tenant from opening another store within a certain radius of the leased premises.

Purpose

The purpose is to prevent tenant from opening other nearby stores that would siphon away sales, causing a decrease in percentage rent. Landlord's remedies in the event tenant does open a store within the radius can include adding the sales figures from the other store or stores to the sales figure for the leased premises.

Radius Distance Can Depend on Population Density

The radius distance under the restriction can vary depending on the leverage of the tenant and the geographic region in which the store operates. A strong national tenant may be able to negotiate a short radius or, in some cases, the deletion of the restriction entirely. Depending on where the store is located, the radius could be a quarter mile or five miles. In a high density urban setting, a shorter radius restriction is more

Radius restrictions should be reviewed against future growth plans.

appropriate. In a less dense suburban or small city setting, a second store even a few miles away may draw potential customers and associated sales.

Other Radius Considerations

To determine if a radius restriction is acceptable, a prospective tenant needs to think through a few things:

What is the growth plan for the business? If the intent is to expand the company's presence in the particular geographic area, a radius restriction may be problematic. The growth plan for five years from now may be hard to gauge with any accuracy. However, the tenant should give this some thought. If there is a chance of potential store growth, the radius should be shortened as much as possible.

As part of tenant's due diligence when negotiating the lease, the tenant should look at the map of the area around the store. This may be obvious, but it is worth the time to look at the map to get a sense of the intersections and retail areas within the radius zone. Is there potential for new retail development? Is the area poised for rapid growth or change? These types of factors should be considered in the radius length.

Also, is the radius distance as the crow flies, or is it by street distance? This will help provide an understanding of the potential area within the radius restriction.

Some radius restriction provisions will try to apply the restriction not only to tenant but also very broadly to any entity that controls, is controlled by, or is under common control with tenant, as well as any partner, officer, director or stockholder of tenant that may have a financial interest in tenant. The prospective tenant needs to consider this, particularly if tenant is owned by investors that also own other companies. A private equity company that invests in a variety of companies, including tenant, may have a potential problem with such a broad provision.

CHAPTER TWENTY

CO-TENANCY

Not all retail tenants can get a landlord to agree to a co-tenancy provision, but this still should be part of the tenant's discussion with its broker or landlord.

A co-tenancy provision allows a tenant to delay opening or to pay a reduced amount of rent when certain conditions are not met. This can be triggered both before the store opens and also once the store is operating. Usually, the condition is that certain other stores, such as anchors, or a certain percentage of stores in the center have to be open for business. For example, if a certain anchor tenant plus 70% of the remaining space in the center is not open for business, then the co-tenancy provision could be triggered.

The remedy if tenant is not yet open for business can be either a delay in store opening without penalty or opening and operating at a reduced rent. If tenant already is open, the tenant's remedy usually is a reduction in rent during the period in which the co-tenancy requirement is not met. Tenant also can negotiate a termination right if the co-tenancy matter is not cured within a certain period of time, such as 180 days.

The reason for a co-tenancy provision is that a tenant is spending a lot of money for a particular site and center, and if that center is not operating as it should, then tenant should receive a remedy. By negotiating this provision into a lease, a tenant will protect itself in case other stores close or fail to open as planned.

The co-tenancy provision can be very effective protection for a tenant that is leasing space in a shopping center in large part because of the customer traffic it may receive from neighboring tenants. Tenant is paying a premium rent for this high profile tenant mix and should have a remedy if landlord is unable or unwilling to provide it.

CHAPTER TWENTY ONE

NON DISTURBANCE AND NO BUILD AREA

As discussed previously, the retail tenant should have the right to dictate the aesthetic conditions of the exterior store front, as well as the interior of the store. This is important because the appearance of the store will help maximize customer traffic and will tie into the tenant's marketing and branding efforts.

In addition to control the aesthetics of the exterior storefront, a retail tenant should be concerned with the common area of the center adjacent to its store and with the visibility and access of the store to the main streets adjoining the center.

No Build Zone

The tenant should insist upon a provision in the lease prohibiting landlord from making any changes in the common areas immediately in front of the store. This would include restricting installation of structures or other improvements like kiosks, signs or automated teller machines. A retail tenant does not want to have its store blocked in any way by these types of items and does not want to have interference with potential customer traffic.

**Imagine a critical meeting with your biggest client with
the sound of drilling coming from the floor above.**

Visibility and Access

The landlord should covenant that it will not make any changes that would reduce the visibility of the leased premises from any adjacent street or reduce access to and from the leased premises. The goal for the tenant is to prohibit any landlord activity that might interfere with customer car or foot traffic to its store. The parking in the center should be in compliance with applicable law.

Non-Disturbance and Construction Activities

The tenant can negotiate a remedy in the event landlord unreasonably interferes with tenant's operation. One possible remedy is to have a rent abatement in the event any construction work by landlord, or authorized by landlord, unreasonably interferes with the tenant's business operations or use of the leased premises. This type of remedy affords the tenant an immediate fix for the interference and interruption in the business or store operations. It also provides a strong incentive for landlord to resolve the interference and interruption, which further benefits the tenant.

CHAPTER TWENTY TWO

INSURANCE

Tenant should anticipate that the lease will require it to maintain general liability and property casualty insurance during the term. This provision is as much for tenant's benefit as it is for landlord's. Insurance provisions are technical, use and location specific, and often subject to changes that the insurance industry regularly makes to the types of insurance that are ordinarily available.

That said, there are a few broad comments that can be made regarding insurance. The rest should be discussed with an experienced lawyer when the actual lease is being negotiated. Those few broad comments are:

Talk to Your Insurance Representative Early

This often is overlooked, but, as mentioned before, your insurance agent or risk manager should be brought into the lease process early. The best way to handle this is to cut and paste the insurance section of the lease right into an email to your agent. Having the agent review the terms and provide feedback will help you know what conflicts there are between your policy and the requirements of the lease. Handling this early will avoid any last-minute problems before you are ready to sign.

Insurance Certificates

A tenant should be prepared to provide a certificate of insurance to landlord prior to tenant's taking possession of the leased premises.

Landlord Compromise

A landlord's attorney might claim that it is restricted from changing the insurance provisions due to covenants under their loan agreements. However, when pushed, the landlord's risk manager usually will find room to compromise. It is critical to negotiate this early in the process. If the insurance is left to the end of the negotiation, tenant may not have enough time or leverage to modify the provisions.

Waiver of Subrogation

The parties should insert a mutual waiver of subrogation with respect to property casualty. An experience lawyer can explain the reasoning and details, but the prospective tenant should be aware of this and should raise it with its lawyer.

Casualty Issues

A tenant should raise two specific items with its attorney and risk manager and have them discuss these with their landlord counterparts: a) who is insuring the improvements within the leased premises and b) should tenant obtain business interruption insurance? Sometimes the landlord will obtain these types of insurance, and tenant might be paying for them through the common area maintenance charge. Not only would it be a waste of money for both landlord and tenant to obtain this insurance, but it could lead to complication if two insurance companies are insuring for the same thing.

The insurance section should be negotiated early in the lease process, and the negotiation should include the risk managers of landlord and tenant. If landlord and tenant leave the insurance negotiation only to their lawyers, they might end up with an insurance section that appears legally sound but is practically useless. If insurance is left as the last open issue in a lease, the looming deadline pressures could lead to an unnecessarily difficult negotiation.

CHAPTER TWENTY THREE

ASSIGNMENT AND SUBLEASING

The assignment and sublease provision rarely has an immediate impact on a tenant at the time it signs its lease. As a result, tenants sometimes do not think through this lease section carefully during negotiation. The assignment and sublease language becomes very important in a few circumstances, so a tenant should review this section with a consideration toward certain items:

Sublease

- <u>Realistically View Future Business</u>: All tenants sign leases with the expectation that the business will do well at the location. Excitement is high, and the desire generally is to get the lease signed and the business opened as soon as possible. The reality is that the statistics for new businesses are daunting – roughly 80% of new businesses fail within the first two years. The 2009 recession showed that existing businesses can face severe challenges when expanding the number of locations. A sublease and assignment provision should be written to accommodate the needs of a tenant when its business does not do as well as expected.

- <u>Dumping a Losing Location</u>: If a business fails or a site underperforms, a tenant may want to wind down operations and quickly unload the lease obligation. The typical way to do this is to sublease the site to a subtenant. The sublease provision should provide maximum flexibility in the event quick action becomes necessary. Things to look for include minimal restrictions on the type of permitted subtenant, limited landlord approval rights, and a short time period for any landlord review. In conjunction with this, a tenant also should review the permitted use section of the lease to make sure it is as broad as possible, so that prospective subtenants are not prohibited from operating at the site.

Assignment

- <u>Stock and Asset Sales</u>: If a tenant desires to sell its company, it likely will be done by a stock or an asset sale. A stock sale is the sale of the stock of the company (i.e. the buyer steps into the shoes of current management in the existing company). The lease remains unchanged because the tenant does not change. An asset sale is the sale of some or all of the assets of the company to a separate company, which usually results in the formation of a new tenant entity. In an asset sale, the lease is assigned to the new tenant.

- <u>No Landlord Consent</u>: The assignment provision should be written to allow for an assignment in an asset sale to be done either with no landlord consent or with very limited landlord consent. Landlord may insist on certain criteria for the new tenant entity, and these criteria should be reviewed to make sure they are not unnecessarily problematic.

- <u>Change of Control</u>: Selling stock of the company technically is not an assignment, but a careful landlord might identify a significant transfer of stock as a 'change of control' requiring landlord consent. A tenant should try to exclude a company-wide stock sale from the landlord review and consent process. However, if this is not possible, then the review criteria should be checked, similar to the assignment review criteria, to make sure they are not unnecessarily problematic.

Going Public

A tenant that is a private company now but may have a public stock offering in the future should make sure that the act of raising capital by issuing voting stock to the public will not be deemed an assignment or sublease. Listing the tenant company on a national securities exchange should be permitted without landlord's prior approval. This will avoid problems when the tenant will be extremely busy with other issues.

Review Fees

The lease usually will contain a provision requiring tenant to reimburse landlord for landlord's cost to consent to a tenant assignment and sublease. The landlord's first draft of the lease often will have a broad reimbursement provision. A few things to consider: the consent fees can be capped, they could be limited to out-of-pocket third party costs (rather than landlord charging for its own time to review), and they can be limited to legal fees only. The review fee cost often comes as a surprise to tenants who have not bothered to look at the sublease and assignment section until they are in the midst of such a transfer.

A lease is a multi-year commitment, and it is very important to think through the terms not only in light of tenant's present day needs but also for what tenant may need (sometimes urgently) years into the future.

CHAPTER TWENTY FOUR

SNDA'S, ESTOPPELS, AND FINANCIAL STATEMENTS

Most tenants have uncertainty as to exactly what a Subordination, Non-Disturbance, and Attornment Agreement (SNDA) is - probably because of its lengthy name - but it is very useful in the event a landlord is having trouble meeting its debt obligations.

Subordination, Non-Disturbance, and Attornment Agreements

A SNDA is three things in one agreement: (1) Tenant agrees to subordinate its leasehold interest to the interest of landlord's lender, (2) landlord's lender agrees that, so long as tenant fulfills its obligations under the lease, tenant's leasehold interest will not be disturbed, and (3) tenant agrees that, in the event the landlord's lender steps into the shoes of landlord through a landlord loan default, then tenant will recognize lender as the new landlord. This agreement helps to provide certainty in the event a landlord is unable to meet its debt obligation and landlord's lender exercises its default remedies.

A well-represented tenant will typically either ask for a SNDA agreement during the negotiation process or have the lease state that a landlord will obtain one upon tenant's request. Also, landlord should use

Since commercial properties are landlord investments, tenants should expect SNDAs and estoppels during the term.

dilligent efforts to receive a non-disturbance agreement from any future lenders. An agreement like this should provide comfort to a tenant during landlord financial problems and will enable a tenant to maintain its focus on its business and not be distracted by lease issues.

Estoppels

An estoppel may be requested by the landlord from time to time if the landlord takes out a loan against the property or refinances a loan. It also may arise if landlord is selling the property. It usually must be returned within a certain period of time, such as ten days.

The estoppel simply is a form requesting tenant to acknowledge certain lease terms, including the lease term dates and the rent amount. The estoppel will also request the tenant to state if there are any defaults or other issues with the lease or landlord. The tenant should be diligent in answering the provisions because if the tenant has any issues with the lease or landlord, these issues should be reflected in the estoppel.

Financial Statements

Unless the retail or corporate tenant has a strong national reputation, landlord more likely than not will require tenant to provide financial statements from time to time. This likely would arise in a financing or sale of the center. Generally, this provision is not too problematic, but the tenant should be aware of a few things. The tenant should be required to provide only the most recently available statements and should not be obligated to prepare new financial statements to fulfill landlord's request.

Landlord should be limited to requesting financial statements to not more than once per year, to avoid unnecessarily burdening tenant. Tenant should be able to have the financial statements certified as accurate by an officer or authorized representative, rather than having them certified by an independent accountant. Including these restrictions regarding the financial statements will prevent administrative emergencies or problems for tenant.

CHAPTER TWENTY FIVE

ANTICIPATING LANDLORD PROBLEMS

If a landlord appears to be having operational problems or it is likely that landlord will soon, it is important to have a few defensive provisions to protect tenant.   Landlord difficulties might manifest themselves in a variety of ways – a decreased maintenance level in the center, delays in repairs or maintenance, or even rumors of possible landlord loan problems.   If the landlord appears to be having its own difficulty, then these tenant protections may greatly help the tenant through such landlord difficulties.

In a booming economy, a tenant may not be concerned with its landlord's condition. Vacancies may be low, rents high, and negotiating leverage in landlord's favor. However, during an economic downturn or recession, such as from 2008-2010, tenants need to be acutely aware of the financial condition of a landlord. A foreclosure by landlord's lender may not directly impact a tenant, but it will be a distraction that the tenant cannot afford as it rides out the same economic downturn.

Some defensive provisions for the tenant include the following:

Self Help

Self-help provides a tenant the right to fulfill landlord's lease obligations if the landlord does not do them and then deduct the cost from rent. A self help provision can be very valuable to a tenant. It provides a tenant with a right to act on behalf of a landlord in the event the landlord fails to do what it is required to do under the lease. For example, if landlord is required to keep the roof in a water-tight and leak free condition but fails to do so, then tenant would have the right to exercise self help. This self help would be repairing the roof and offsetting the cost of doing so against future rent.

A self-help provision will avoid a situation in which a tenant is held hostage to the problems of a landlord when landlord fails to act. Self help also may help a tenant remedy the problem in a timely manner, avoid protracted negotiations with a non-acting landlord, and incur possible legal fees to enforce lease obligations. Ultimately, defensive provisions like this will allow a tenant to stay focused on its business and productivity.

Rent Abatement

A rent abatement provision provides for rent abatement if landlord fails to fulfill its lease obligations after a certain waiting period. Not every landlord will agree to a tenant's ideal rent abatement provision. However, it is a very useful tenant right, so some version of the provision should be included.

A rent abatement provision simply provides tenant with an automatic rent abatement in the event the landlord fails to timely do what it is obligated to do under the lease. For example, if landlord is obligated to provide utility service and the service is interrupted for 48 hours, then rent would automatically abate if landlord does not fix the problem within the 48 hours. A secondary right would allow tenant to terminate the lease if this issue is not cured within 30 days. Although a landlord will want to soften this language, it is a very good provision to have for a tenant because the mere threat of the rent abatement usually is enough to motivate a landlord to fulfill its lease obligations.

Ultimately, defensive provisions like these will provide a tenant with protections in case landlord either experiences problems or becomes willfully combative. A lease needs to be designed to allow tenant to maintain an unfettered focus on its business operations, and these tenant rights will help to minimize any disturbances that could be catastrophic without a quick remedy.

CHAPTER TWENTY SIX

LANDLORD DEFAULT

The prior chapter discussed tenant remedies for landlord's performance problems. These remedies include self help and rent abatement.

A lease also could contain a landlord default provision. This provision would provide for the terms under which landlord would be in default in the lease. Typically, this provision would state that landlord is in default in the event it does not cure the lease breach within thirty days of notice.

The provision also would provide that, for breaches that cannot be cured within thirty days, no default will occur so long as landlord commences the cure within thirty days and diligently completes the cure. If tenant has received landlord's lender contact information, tenant normally is required to notify the lender of the default as well.

A landlord default can be challenging for a tenant. The tenant desires a remedy, but the tenant likely does not want to spend money in litigation enforcing its right to damages. A tenant also probably does not want to terminate the lease and walk away from the site. The tenant will have invested time, money, and resources to this location, and terminating the lease will come at the cost of losing this investment.

A wise tenant will have the self help and rent abatement remedies built into the lease so that it can exercise those and continue operations as smoothly as possible. The default usually is reserved for more catastrophic situations in which the landlord is grossly inept or virtually non-functional. When things are irreparably bad, a tenant may decide to cut itself loose from the lease and walk away. At that point, the landlord default provision is an effective way to document the default, to terminate the lease, and to establish the basis for seeking damages in court.

CHAPTER TWENTY SEVEN

INDEMNIFICATION AND RELEASES

The indemnification, release, casualty, condemnation sections are highly technical and are somewhat dependent on the law of the state which contains the leased premises.

Indemnification

The exact language for the indemnification will depend on the individual state law. The lease ideally should contain mutual indemnifications between landlord and tenant that exclude the negligence and willful misconduct of the other party.

The landlord may want tenant to indemnify the landlord even in cases in which the landlord is negligent. The basis for landlord's position regarding this usually is that the tenant's insurance should still apply even in cases of the landlord's negligence. However, in some states, any lease provision that relieves the landlord from liability arising from the landlord's negligence is void. Therefore, it is important to check the relevant state law on this topic to make sure there is a good understanding of both how the law governs this topic and what insurance needs to be obtained.

Releases

The release section also must be reviewed in light of applicable state law. Often, the tenant is responsible for injuries that happen in the leased premises due to a defect, and landlord is not responsible. As with an indemnification provision, lease provisions that exculpate the landlord from liability due to its own negligence are void under certain state laws.

The law of the applicable state also should be checked to see if landlord is liable for injuries or damage in the leased premises due to latent defects, concealed conditions, a nuisance or violation of law, and any failure to reasonably repair the leased premises. The landlord already may attempt to address these items in the lease by pushing the burden onto the tenant, but an understanding of the applicable state law can help when reviewing this provision.

Finally, the parties should agree to a mutual waiver of subrogation. This is beneficial to the tenant as the landlord will waive its right against the tenant for property casualty. The tenant more likely will be the cause of the casualty than the landlord. This is the case because the tenant is occupying the leased premises on a day-to-day basis and the landlord is not. A mutual waiver of subrogation typically is not a problem to include in the lease as the insurance companies generally accept them in current leases.

CHAPTER TWENTY EIGHT

CASUALTY AND CONDEMNATION

Casualty

In the event a casualty occurs, the repair and restoration terms, and tenant's rights generally, need to offer a clear path to a quick resolution.

Leases tend to follow the same general terms in the casualty section:

- If there is a fire or other casualty that prevents the leased premises from being used in part or in whole and the landlord reasonably believes the premises can be repaired within a certain amount of time, such as 180 days, then landlord should have the right to repair and restore the premises. Landlord should diligently make these repairs to completion.

- If there is a fire or other casualty that cannot be repaired within a certain amount of time, such as 180 days, tenant should have the right to terminate the lease.

**Casualty provisions should be reviewed carefully,
as some properties are more complex than others.**

- In the event that more than fifty percent of the value of the property is damaged or destroyed by fire or other casualty, then landlord can have the option to terminate the lease.

- Landlords generally will not agree to repair or restore any equipment or trade fixtures installed by a tenant.

- The landlord should agree to provide property casualty insurance equal to the replacement cost value of the building. The landlord also should maintain general liability coverage.

- During any period in which the leased premises cannot be used by tenant, the rent should abate in proportion to the amount of the leased premises that cannot be used for tenant's business. Some landlord may try to insert a clause stating that the rent will not abate if tenant causes, or negligently causes, the damage. However, if tenant is paying for the landlord's business interruption insurance as additional rent, then tenant should be able to avail itself of that insurance and receive the rent abatement. This is something that should be addressed with each individual lease.

Condemnation

In any condemnation, the tenant should have the right to receive an award for condemnation of the tenant's trade fixtures, equipment, and ancillary items. Landlord will want to make sure that the tenant's award does not diminish the landlord's award.

In a partial condemnation situation, the landlord should restore the leased premises and the building to a functional structure, and rent should abate on a proportionate and fair basis.

CHAPTER TWENTY NINE

DEFAULT

The default section in a lease lists the set of conditions upon which a landlord may terminate a lease or tenant's right to possession and can then seek a remedy. The default remedies are significant and can severely impact a tenant. This section should be reviewed to minimize the risk that landlord will be able to ever put tenant in default and seek a remedy.

Default Might Be Easily Triggered

The default provisions typically will say that a default occurs in the event tenant fails to pay rent when due or within a few days of when due. Having a few days' buffer is obviously the better of the two versions. However, a tenant should try to require landlord to notify tenant before a default can occur.

Landlord to Notify Before Default

An ideal default provision would include this notice requirement. The default provision would then state something to the effect of "An event of default will occur in the event tenant fails to pay rent within five days after receipt of landlord's notice."

Soften the Default Trigger for Administrative Problems

A notice requirement like this would prevent a potential default if tenant has an administrative problem and fails to timely pay rent. Some companies may pay rent through autopay, but expanding companies may not have the established systems in place. For example, a rapidly growing company that may have organizational challenges as part of its growing pains would probably be helped very much by having the default for late rent be triggered "five days after notice from landlord" and not "five days from when due".

Limit to Two Times in 12 Months

Landlords very likely will refuse to accept this type of provision. It essentially allows a tenant to be perpetually late with payment obligations. It also shifts the obligation of rent payment from tenant to landlord, who then is burdened with collecting it. A compromise position is to allow the notice provision but to limit the provision to two times in any twelve month period.

Time to Diligently Cure

A default for any tenant requirement other than rent payment typically is thirty days after landlord's notice. For tenant matters that cannot be cured within 30 days, it is helpful to state that a default will not occur so long as tenant commences to cure the matter within thirty days of notice and diligently completes the cure.

When a tenant is about to sign a lease, it usually is focused optimistically on the best case scenario for the new premises. It envisions a successful business in a problem-free environment. However, by taking some time to review the lease provisions, including the default section, that address what can happen when problems arise, a tenant can protect itself when the unexpected occurs. It is important to confirm that the default section is reviewed with respect to the individual tenant's business to avoid issues that may distract the tenant from its business objectives.

CHAPTER THIRTY

HOLDOVER

In my fifteen years of experience handling about 700 leases, there has only been one instance in which the holdover provision was triggered. It remains, however, an important provision to protect a tenant at the end of the lease term.

A holdover provision provides landlord a remedy in the event the tenant remains in the leased premises, or 'holds over,' after the end of the lease term. The holdover provision will provide landlord remedies in the event the tenant does not timely vacate by the end of the term.

Holdover Remedy

Landlords typically will require tenants to pay 200% of the most recent base rent and be liable for ancillary damages. A landlord also may deem the holdover as a renewal of the term on a month-to-month, or in some cases a year-to-year, basis.

A diligent tenant usually can negotiate the holdover rent to be 125-150% of the most recent base rent. A tenant should aim to keep the holdover provision to the smallest penalty as possible. An ideal provision would have holdover rent at 125% of base rent and no liability for consequential damages.

Ancillary Damages

If the landlord is adamant about keeping tenant liable for ancillary damages for the holdover, one reasonable compromise to consider is a provision providing that tenant initially is only liable for holdover rent (ideally, at 125%), but in the event landlord has a new tenant ready to occupy the same space and tenant then does not vacate within 30 days of notice from landlord, the tenant then would be liable for actual damages after the 30 days.

No Renewal

Further, the holdover should not be considered a renewal of the term or a typical month-to-month tenancy. A tenant should try to limit the holdover period solely to any period after the term's expiration during which the tenant is actually occupying the space. Once the tenant vacates the space, the holdover period should end. A diligent landlord may want the holdover period and rent obligation to run the full month-to-month period.

Is Landlord Liable for Late Delivery?

While a tenant is reviewing the holdover provision, it is a good idea to compare tenant's liability for holding over with landlord's liability for a late delivery. If there is limited liability to a landlord for delivering late, it should not have a strong argument for a severe holdover provision because it likely is not exposed to much liability with respect to a future tenant. However, if landlord does have a severe consequence for late delivery, including rent credits or a tenant termination right, the tenant should expect that the landlord will want a strong holdover provision as an effective enforcement mechanism to get the tenant out of the premises at the end of the term.

A holdover provision might be used rarely in actual day-to-day leasing, but taking the time to review what may happen at the end of the term, which may be 5 or 10 or 15 years from the present, will help to ensure a smooth experience for the entire tenancy.

CHAPTER THIRTY ONE

MISCELLANEOUS LEASE PROVISIONS

There almost always is a section at the end of a lease labeled 'Miscellaneous' into which shorter provisions that do not warrant their own section are dumped. Do not let the 'Miscellaneous' label or the random assortment of topics fool you. These are important, and each one should be reviewed carefully.

In no particular order, here is a brief discussion of four topics that usually appear in this section:

Attorney's Fees

A lease should contain a 'prevailing party' provision regarding attorney's fees. In the event of a dispute between landlord and tenant that results in litigation or other action, this provision would require the losing party to pay the winning party's legal fees. The purpose of this is to encourage the parties to resolve disputes quickly and to prevent unnecessary litigation.

For a tenant with a growing business, this can be invaluable because it prevents a landlord with deeper resources from bullying a tenant. Without this provision, a landlord could shirk its maintenance and operation duties because it knows the tenant might be less likely to incur the costs of litigation. If a tenant clearly is in the right, a landlord also will be less likely to engage in a battle of attrition in litigation because it knows it will have to pay for this strategy.

Notices

It is worth looking at the legal notice section, which states how one party can sending notices to the other, to make sure that the process will be practical for tenant's business. First, the notice address should be checked to make sure it is correct. Should the notice go to the store or the factory or the corporate headquarters? Second, is the method of delivery practical? Faxes are fairly outdated. Overnight delivery is very useful. Some parties prefer email, but despite the virtual certainty of delivery, emails can get lost in inboxes. It is worth spending two minutes to think through this before the lease is signed.

Broker's Fees

Landlord typically pays broker commissions for both landlord's broker and tenant's broker, and the lease should state this. There also should be a mutual indemnity between landlord and tenant for any other brokers or parties claiming a commission.

Rules and Regulations

A lease often will list the rules and regulations of the building or center, and these may be attached as an exhibit. Spend a few minutes to review the rules to see if there are any issues. Can tenant operate a coffee maker or a small kitchen? What are the rules on trash storage? The rules and any future changes by landlord should be held to a reasonable standard. The rules also should be enforced equally among all tenants in the center or building.

By spending a few minutes reviewing the 'Miscellaneous' section, a prospective tenant can ensure that problems will be minimized during the day-to-day operations in the leased premises. This is important as it will allow tenant to focus on its business and not on disputes with landlord.

CHAPTER THIRTY TWO

THE CUSTOMER IN-STORE EXPERIENCE

I spoke at the Outdoor Retailer Summer and Winter Markets in Salt Lake City in 2010 and 2013 about the unique store operation concerns that outdoor retailers have. Outdoor retailers and certain other retailers have a unique focus on the customer in-store experience, both as a way to compete against online competition and as another strategy to boost store sales. These retailers might consider the following items as part of store experience:

Retail vs. Storeroom Rent

Outdoor retailers and other with large products may need significant storage for inventory. While some retailers can place virtually all of their product on the showroom floor, outdoor retailers and others may need basements or other storage areas to house bikes, kayaks, and other large items. If the storage area is large, consider negotiating a reduced rent in your lease for these areas. Retail rents typically are priced on the assumption that almost the entire space will be used as sales area.

**Tenants focusing on the customer experience need to
evaluate their leases to maximize the opportunities.**

Store Hours

Outdoor customers may have unique shopping hours. Fly
fisherman and cyclists may want early morning hours. Running groups
and weekend warriors may want evening hours. Consider negotiating
customer-friendly store hours into your lease.

Window Displays

Showing your product in store windows may be a critical component to driving customer traffic. Make sure your lease permits maximum flexibility for window displays.

Workshops and In-Store Events

Many retailers are using in-store workshops and events to avoid losing market share to the internet. A tenant needs to confirm that their lease and applicable zoning permit these types of events. In addition, the retailer should check with the local municipality to make sure it obtains any necessary license for workshops and similar marketing tools.

Parking Lot Product Demonstrations

Having the right to use the adjacent parking area for product demonstrations can be a critical sales strategy for outdoor retailers. Customers are much more likely to become interested in the bikes, tents, boats, and other outdoor products when they are easy to see, touch, and test. Securing the right to use the parking lot for sales, demonstrations, or seasonal exhibits can be a great sales approach.

Unique Environmental Concerns

Outdoor retailers often sell products that have unique environmental issues. Camping fuel, bike lubricant and cleaners, and waterproof patch kits are three products that may be restricted hazardous material under a lease. It is important to consider the types of products being sold in the store. Any environmental issues then can be addressed specifically in the lease.

Liability Insurance

As with all leases, the insurance provision should be checked to make sure it is appropriate for the specific business. Product liability, in-store workshops, outdoor demonstrations, and customer product testing are just some of the items unique to outdoor retailers that should be covered by insurance.

Floor Load and Product Weight

Some outdoor retailer products may be unusually heavy. If weight is an issue, the outdoor retailer should make sure that the heavy products will not violate the floor load limits in both the lease and the actual store.

Co-Tenancy

If your retail store is dependent on customers from adjacent stores (e.g. your store is in the same center as a Whole Foods, and you want the benefit of the Whole Foods customer traffic) consider negotiating a co-tenancy provision, which allows a tenant to pay reduced rent if certain other stores in the same center are not open for business. This is a technical lease term, but one to consider.

Exclusive Use

If having a competitor in the same center would be detrimental to your business, consider negotiating an exclusive use provision in your lease for either the type of store or particular products. An exclusive use right would prevent losing business to a nearby competitor.

This is just a short review of very important lease terms a retailer should consider in its leases if it is focusing on the customer experience in the store. Provisions like these can be technical, and an experience lawyer can help to negotiate them.

APPENDIX

LEASE CHECKLIST FORM

1. <u>Landlord</u>: Entity should be named correctly and in good standing.

2. <u>Tenant</u>: Entity should be correctly named and in good standing.

3. <u>Property</u>: To be correctly and specifically identified.

4. <u>Leased Premises</u>: To be correctly and specifically identified. Square footage to be correctly stated. The rentable area should be verified.

5. <u>Term</u>: Confirm it is for the proper duration.

6. <u>Renewal Options</u>: If applicable, confirm they are stated for the proper duration.

7. Rent Commencement Date: Confirm it is correctly stated or calculated and that tenant is not obligated to pay rent until the premises is ready for occupancy.

8. Early Termination Rights: If any, confirm they are properly stated, with the correct termination fee.

9. Annual Rent: Confirm this is correctly stated. If based on a dollar per square foot basis, the rent will adjust if the square footage adjusts.

10. Percentage Rent: Ensure this is clearly calculated based on the correct breakpoint, with the payment requirements confirmed as appropriate.

11. Proportionate Share: This is to be calculated with rentable area of the building as the denominator and not just the area currently leased.

12. Additional Rent: Confirm this is clearly stated in accordance with the agreed-upon terms. Certain taxes and common area expenses are to be excluded.

13. Utilities: Confirm who is to arrange for utilities and who is to pay.

14. Co-Tenancy: If included, confirm the co-tenancy trigger and remedy complies with the agreed-upon terms.

15. Landlord's Construction: Confirm this matches the understanding of tenant's construction manager.

16. Tenant Construction Allowance: Confirm this matches the deal terms, including when it should be paid by landlord.

17. Condition of Premises at Delivery: This should be clearly stated in the lease, including premises delivery and compliance with law.

18. Tenant's Work: Confirm tenant's work with tenant's construction manager. Ensure tenant's work does not include work that should be a landlord obligation.

19. Landlord's Maintenance and Repair Obligations: Confirm landlord is obligated for structural repairs and common area maintenance.

20. Permitted Use of Premises: Confirm the permitted uses include tenant's intended use.

21. Guarantor(s): If required, make sure that a guarantor's obligation only kicks in after a tenant default.

22. Security Deposit: This should be returned, less any retainage, within 30 days of lease termination.

23. Exclusive Use Rights: If applicable, this should match the agreed-upon deal terms.

24. Radius Restriction: If applicable, confirm this matches tenant's understanding.

25. Assignment and Subletting Rights: Landlord's consent should not be unreasonably withheld, conditioned, or delayed.

26. Visibility and Access: For a retail tenant, confirm that the visibility and access that the premises enjoys at the beginning of the term will not materially change.

27. Signage Rights: Confirm that tenant's storefront and pylon signage matches the tenant's understanding.

28. Common Area Maintenance Requirements: Landlord should maintain the common areas, and the maintenance can be tied to a certain standard.

29. <u>Default</u>: Ideally, a default will not occur until tenant receives written notice from landlord.

30. <u>Brokers</u>: Landlord should pay all broker commissions.

31. <u>Tenant's Insurance</u>: Tenant's insurance manager or agent should review the insurance to confirm acceptable.

32. <u>Disturbance Remedy</u>: If services are disrupted to the extent that tenant cannot operate in the premises, tenant should receive a rent abatement after 48 hours and a termination right after 30 days.

CONCLUSION

A lease agreement generally is a tricky document to negotiate even in the most ordinary of circumstances. A lease requires the parties to negotiate binding terms in the present that will bind landlord and tenant for many years into the future. It requires the parties to be able both to think through and anticipate a variety of circumstances and scenarios that may arise in the future and then to address them now in the agreement.

One important way a company can protect itself, however, is by using an experienced leasing attorney to help review and negotiate the document. With a lawyer's help, one can begin to think through these complex issues and to anticipate the variables.

This is particularly true for those new issues, some unforeseen, arising from the current economy. By taking into consideration the issues discussed above, a tenant will be able to more suitably protect itself under one of its biggest business obligations.

Ideally, this analysis during the lease negotiation process will keep the company's focus away from any problems associated with the lease and on its most important goal: the success of its business.

###

DISCLAIMER

The information contained in this publication is provided for informational purposes only and should not be construed as legal advice on any subject matter and is not guaranteed to be correct, complete, or up-to-date.

No recipients of content from this publication, clients or otherwise, should act or refrain from acting on the basis of any content included in this publication without seeking the appropriate legal or other professional advice on the particular facts and circumstances at issue from an attorney licensed in the recipient's state or otherwise. The content of this publication contains general information and may not reflect current legal developments, verdicts or settlements. James P. Moorhead and the Moorhead Law Group, LLC expressly disclaim all liability in respect to actions taken or not taken based on any or all of the contents of this publication.

☐   ☐ This publication, in part or in whole, and/or any communication with James P. Moorhead or the Moorhead Law Group, LLC do not constitute or create an attorney-client relationship between the Moorhead Law Group, LLC and any other party in any way whatsoever unless and until a Moorhead Law Group, LLC attorney has specifically advised the particular party that the firm is accepting an engagement on its behalf and after appropriate conflicts checks and inquiries have been conducted and an executed engagement letter has been executed and returned to the firm by said party.

☐☐ The owner of this publication is an attorney licensed to practice in Illinois. In some jurisdictions, portions of this publication may be considered advertising. This publication is not intended to be advertising. James P. Moorhead and the Moorhead Law Group, LLC do not wish to represent anyone desiring representation based upon their receipt and review of any portion of this publication that does not comply with legal or ethical rules in those states. Past results afford no guarantee of future results. Every case is different and must be judged on its own merits.

Materials in this publication may not be reproduced in part or in whole without the prior written consent of the owner. To the extent the state bar rules in an individual reader's jurisdiction require Moorhead Law Group, LLC to designate a principal office and/or a single attorney responsible for this publication, Moorhead Law Group, LLC designates its office in Chicago, Illinois, USA as its principal office and designates James P. Moorhead as the attorney responsible for this publication.

www.ingramcontent.com/pod-product-compliance
Lightning Source LLC
Chambersburg PA
CBHW020916180526
45163CB00007B/2755